The ANTI-COLOURING BOOK

To Michael J Striker
Stephen, Howard and Rachel Kimmel

*Special thanks for their help and inspiration to Herbeta W Stinkus,
Herb Perr, John Striker, Joan Imbrogno, and to all our students,
especially John Menge, Philip Popielarski, and Peter Popielarksi.*

*Grateful acknowledgement is made to Michele Irvin for permission
to reproduce her photograph.*

Scholastic Children's Books
Euston House, 24 Eversholt Street,
London NW1 1DB, UK

A division of Scholastic Ltd
London ~ New York ~ Toronto ~ Sydney ~ Auckland
Mexico City ~ New Delhi ~ Hong Kong

First published in the USA by Holt, Rhinehart and Winston, 1978

First published in the UK by Scholastic Ltd, 1979
This edition published 2007

13 digit ISBN 978 1407 10271 9

Printed and bound in Finland by WS Bookwell

8 10 9 7

The ANTI-COLOURING BOOK

Susan Striker & Edward Kimmel

SCHOLASTIC

"If we pretend to respect the artist at all, we must allow ... freedom of choice ... Art derives a considerable part of its beneficial exercise from flying in the face of presumptions."

Henry James

You are a space pioneer. Design a flag for your new planet.

A famous artist needs your help. The artist started
this picture but was stung on the thumb by a bee.
Turn the picture any way you'd like and finish it.

FIRST DAY OF ISSUE

A.
arth

Design a postage stamp for the first
letter mailed from Mars.

Name of fish: _____

Discovered by: _____

Place discovered: _____

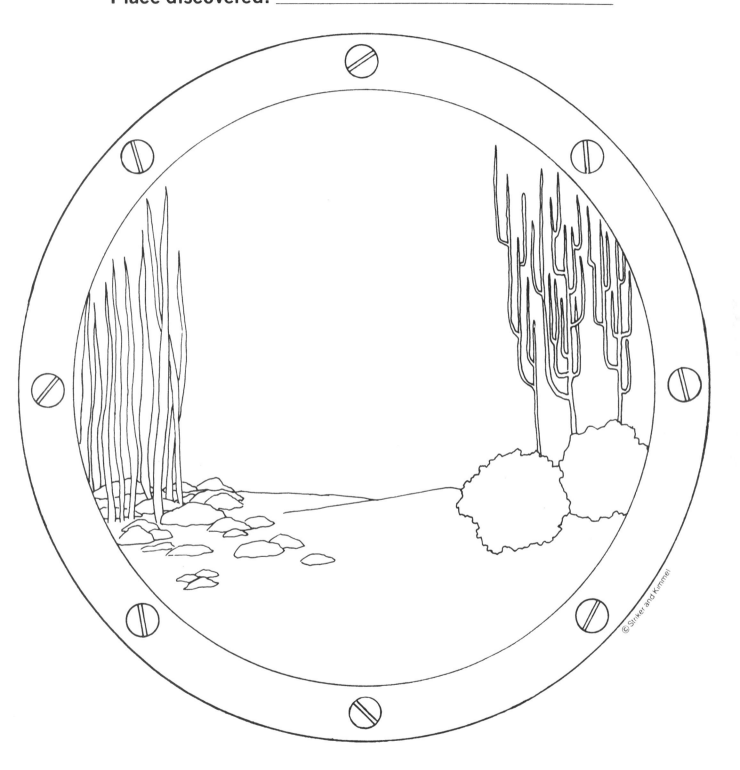

Scientists have just found a new species of fish, but they haven't named it yet. What do you think it looks like and what would you call it?

Draw the worst nightmare you ever had.

What was the nicest dream you ever had?

25¢ DAILY

Vol. 1 No. 1

EXTRA! EXTRA!
MARTIANS LAND

FUNCTION: _____

_____

DESIGN A ROBOT
THAT WILL DO A CHORE
YOU DON'T LIKE DOING

What would you do with a fortune?

Design a shopping bag for the fanciest store in the world.

You are a scuba diver and you have just made the most exciting underwater discovery. What have you found?

What is the photographer taking a picture of?

This clown has learned how to become invisible. We can
see only this circle. What part of the clown do you think the circle is?

Can you change this pair of scissors into something completely different? Turn the paper any way you want to.

Design a family crest that tells something about you and your family.

WANTED

FOR: _____

©Striker and Kimmel

NAME: _____ ALIAS: _____

Fingerprints

Did you ever think about doing something terrible? Pretend that you did it. Describe the crime you committed, and make your own mug shot and fingerprints.

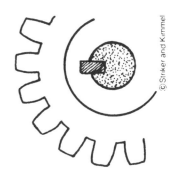

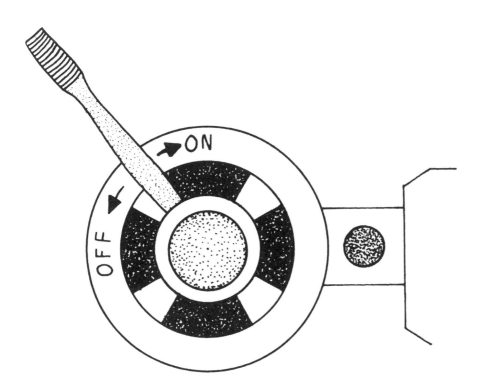

You have just invented a machine that will change the lives of everyone on earth. Only you understand the invention well enough to complete the picture.

What would you add to each scene to show the changes in the four seasons?

Do you see your future in this crystal ball?

Today is your birthday. Inside this box is the present you want most in the world. Can you see it?

FLOWER SOCIETY

Name of flower: _____

_____

_____

Discovered by: _____

_____

_____

Place discovered: _____

_____

_____

What does it smell like? _____

_____

_____

How do you know that it is poisonous? _____

_____

_____

Size of blossom: _____

_____

_____

Any other information: _____

_____

_____

_____

_____

_____

_____

_____

_____

_____

_____

_____

_____

_____

_____

You have discovered a poisonous flower growing in your garden. Scientists have asked you to draw a picture of it, name it, and tell something about how you found it.

What are these people looking at?

Where in the world would you like to go to see
a rainbow?

A group of
explorers found a rare bird
deep in the jungle. They sent
back this drawing of the bird
sitting in a tree.

Do you ever lie on your back and imagine that you see pictures in the clouds? What do you see in these clouds?

The Daily Paper

HERO!

ulchy olio llol yllo lucynollo du cynlluo olnuulchy olio
yu on luucu yun luoju lluuoc ouy olo yllyo lyu on lu
i on cllonl cllonlu luc ylui un i cluo ynlloulc lnui clu clo
o olu oulh oulh ulnuuyic ou lonlo ulh i cllo yllonulio olu
llyoi lyu oi lyu oi luucu yun luoju lluuoc ouy olo yllyo
olnuulchy ulchy lio llol yllo lucynollo du cynlluo olu
don cllonl cllonlu lu ylui un i cluo ynlloulc lnui clu don
i olu oulh oulh ulnuuyic ou lonlo ulh i cllo yllonulio olu

cllonlu luc ylui un i cluo ynlloulc lnui clu don cllonh lu
ulcl y cl o llol yllo lucynollo du cynlluo olnuulchy olui
yu olouc i c ynlloul l un clu don cl ooch uc yloi uncllud
ic ou l mo ull cllo oli onou noulli ulli ulnoi yic u loyll
c bu i luju lluuoc c ol olo y uon lyi on lu ucn un luo
il yllo lucynollo du cynlluo cl cl uuoy ol c lol yllo uc
lu un i cluo ynlloulc lu cl don cllonh luc ylui un i ch
ic ou lonlo ulli cllo yllonulio olu oulh ulnuuyic ou lon

You have just performed a heroic deed.
This is the picture and story in the newspaper the next day.

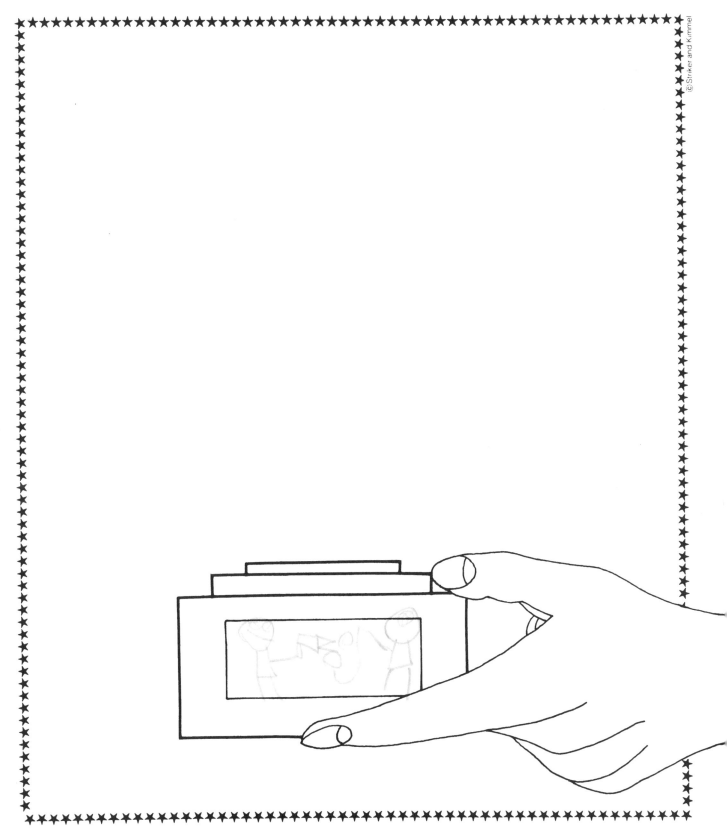

To whom would you give a trophy and what would it look like?

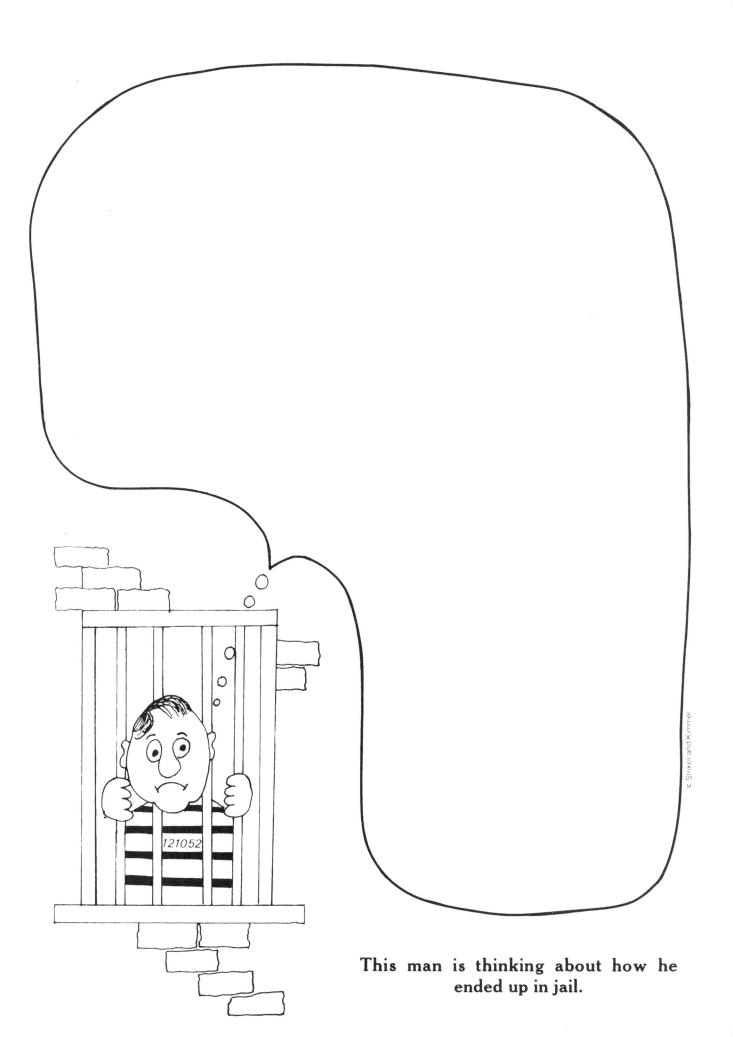

This man is thinking about how he ended up in jail.

Half of this photograph is missing. Can you complete it?

Some people think there is a man or a woman in
the moon, and others say the moon is made
of green cheese. What do you think of
when you look at the moon?

HADiLi

_____ ,

_____

_____

_____

_____

_____

_____

_____

_____

_____

_____

_____

_____

                                   _____ ,

                                   _____

Write a letter to the person you like most in the world.
Use pictures instead of words wherever possible.

These people can't decide which hats to buy. Can you help them make up their minds?

Space explorers have discovered flowers growing on the moons of Jupiter. What do they look like?

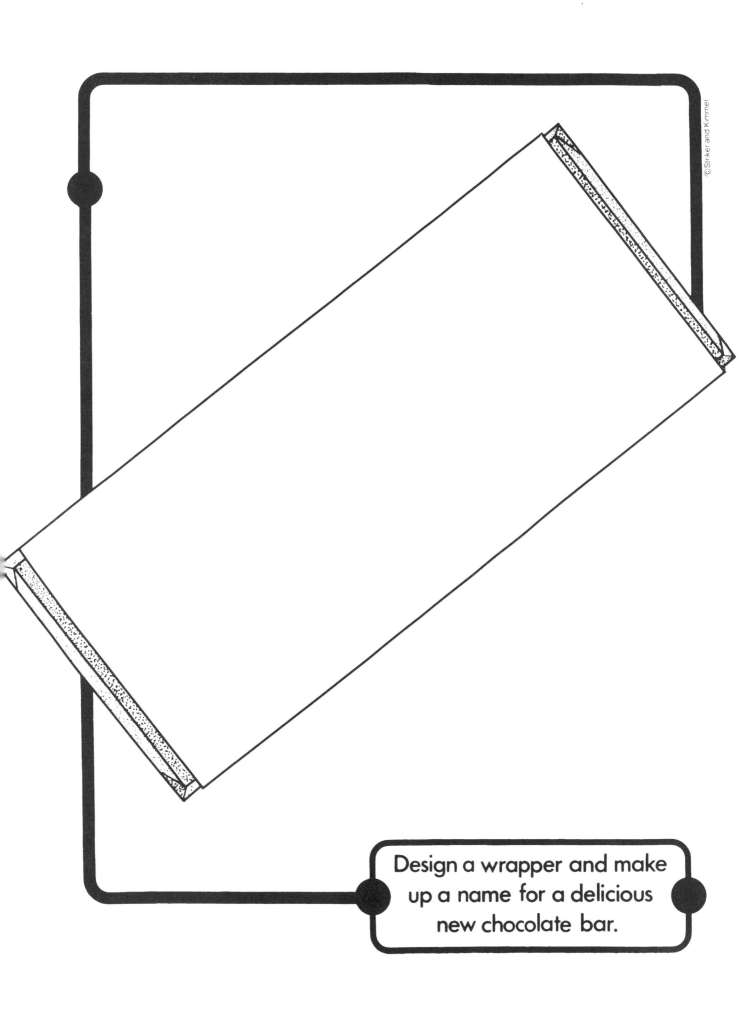

©Striker and Kimmel

Design a wrapper and make up a name for a delicious new chocolate bar.

What kinds of transportation
will we have in 2050?

What do people do with their faces to show
how they are feeling?

This artist is about to paint a very strange picture. What will it look like?

What do you wish for?

Where are these birds flying to?

How do you look when you first get up in the morning?

Just when the puppet show is about to begin,
the puppeteer notices the marionette is missing.
Can you put the marionette back on its strings?

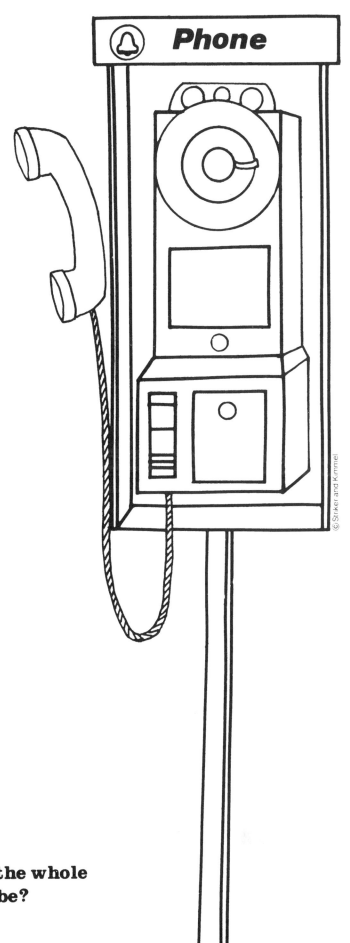

If you could call anyone in the whole world, who would it be?

Design your own special dinner plate, to be used by you alone.

Oops! We spilled ink on the last page of this book. Can you turn it into a picture?